Forces and Motion at the Playground

Stella Graham

REAL LIFE readers™

Rosen Classroom™

New York

Published in 2009 by The Rosen Publishing Group, Inc.
29 East 21st Street, New York, NY 10010

Book Design: Daniel Hosek

Photo Credits: Cover © Grant Faint/The Image Bank/Getty Images; p. 5 © Hirlesteanu Constantin-Ciprian/Shutterstock; pp. 6, 14 (swings) © Stockbyte/Getty Images; pp. 9, 14 (merry-go-round); pp. 10–11, 14 (tug-of-war) © Image Source/Getty Images; pp. 13, 14 (slide) © Jacek Chabraszewski/Shutterstock; p. 14 (soccer) © Amy Myers/Shutterstock; p. 14 (jungle gym) © Sonya Etchison/Shutterstock.

ISBN: 978-1-4358-0057-1
6-pack ISBN: 978-1-4358-0058-8

Manufactured in the United States of America

Contents

Forces and Motion

Force is the power or strength to do something.
A push or a pull is a force.

We can use force to put things in **motion**.
We use force to cause motion every day.
Let's learn about force and motion
at the playground!

Using force and motion at the playground can help you stay healthy.

push

pull

can put things in motion

the power or strength to do something

force

On the Swings

When you push someone on a swing, you use force created by your **muscles**.

This force puts the swing in motion.

If you get in your friend's way, the force of their swinging could knock you over!

When on a swing, you can use the force made by kicking your legs to keep swinging.

The Merry-Go-Round

The merry-go-round is a fun playground ride.
It spins around when you push it.

You use the force of your push to make the merry-go-round move.
The harder you push, the faster the merry-go-round spins. Hang on tight!

The more people that are on a merry-go-round, the heavier it is. That makes it harder to push.

Tug-of-War

You need some friends and a rope to play **tug-of-war**. Form two teams. Each team takes an end of the rope. Both teams pull as hard as they can.

Which team has more force?
The one that can pull the other team toward them has more force.

Down the Slide

A slide needs **gravity** to work.
Gravity is the force that pulls everything toward the ground.
Gravity keeps us on Earth and gives us weight.
When you go down a slide, gravity is the force that puts you in motion.

You need to use the force of your legs to get to the top of a slide. The force of gravity brings you back down.

Time to Play!

Can you think of other ways we use force and motion at the playground?

Glossary

force (FOHRS) The power or strength of something.

gravity (GRA-vuh-tee) The natural force that causes objects to move toward Earth.

motion (MOH-shun) Movement.

muscle (MUH-suhl) A part of the body that makes the body move.

tug-of-war (TUG-UHV-WOHR) A game played by two teams of people pulling a rope in different directions to see who is strongest.

Index

Due to the changing nature of Internet links, The Rosen Publishing Group, Inc., has developed an online list of Web sites related to the subject of this book. This site is updated regularly. Please use this link to access the list: **http://www.rcbmlinks.com/rlr/formo**